MYTHICAL CREATURES

FUSION

THE KRAKEN

by

Rebecca Phillips-Bartlett

BEARPORT PUBLISHING

Minneapolis, Minnesota

Credits
All images are courtesy of Shutterstock.com, unless otherwise specified. With thanks to Getty Images, Thinkstock Photo, iStockphoto, and Adobe Stock.

Recurring – Macrovector, M.KOS. Cover – Daria_Art. 4–5 – tomertu, Morphart Creation. 6–7 – Vega_7, Dan Bagur, Paul Fleet, PrinPrince. 8–9 – Sabelskaya, N. Steele, AlexeyMasliy. 10–11 – Morozov Alexey, Anastelfy. 12–13 – Ajit S N, Nejron Photo, Macrovector, AWSeebaran. 14–15 – lunamarina, Andrey_Kuzmin, Natalllenka.m. 16–17 – Dotted Yeti, Steicha, New Vectors, Daniel Eskridge. 18–19 – Hatteviden, Lubomira08, delcarmat. 20–21 – Peter Hermes Furian, Maryshot, Uking. 22–23 – SergiyN, Hakase_420.

Bearport Publishing Company Product Development Team
Publisher: Jen Jenson; Director of Product Development: Spencer Brinker; Managing Editor: Allison Juda; Editor: Cole Nelson; Associate Editor: Naomi Reich; Associate Editor: Tiana Tran; Art Director: Colin O'Dea; Designer: Kim Jones; Designer: Kayla Eggert; Product Development Specialist: Owen Hamlin

Library of Congress Cataloging-in-Publication Data

Names: Phillips-Bartlett, Rebecca, 1999-, author.
Title: The kraken / by Rebecca Phillips-Bartlett.
Description: Minneapolis, Minnesota : Bearport Publishing Company, [2025] | Series: Mythical creatures | Includes index.
Identifiers: LCCN 2024034565 (print) | LCCN 2024034566 (ebook) | ISBN 9798892327411 (hardcover) | ISBN 9798892327916 (paperback) | ISBN 9798892328289 (ebook)
Subjects: LCSH: Kraken--Juvenile literature.
Classification: LCC QL89.2.K73 P45 2025 (print) | LCC QL89.2.K73 (ebook) | DDC 594/.58--dc23/eng/20240813
LC record available at https://lccn.loc.gov/2024034565
LC ebook record available at https://lccn.loc.gov/2024034566

For more information, write to Bearport Publishing, 5357 Penn Avenue South, Minneapolis, MN 55419.

CONTENTS

MYTHS, MAGIC, AND MORE

Most people have heard of the octopus-like beast known as the kraken (KRA-kuhn). But you probably haven't seen one in real life. Why not? Because the kraken is a **mythical** creature!

For thousands of years, sailors have told stories about the kraken. Different **legends** talk about this creature in different ways. Let's learn what the stories have to say!

Legends of the kraken come from Scandinavia.

WHAT DOES THE KRAKEN LOOK LIKE?

Let's take a closer look at this sea monster.

Arms

In stories, the kraken often has eight arms, like a squid.

Beak

A parrotlike beak is thought to help the kraken feed.

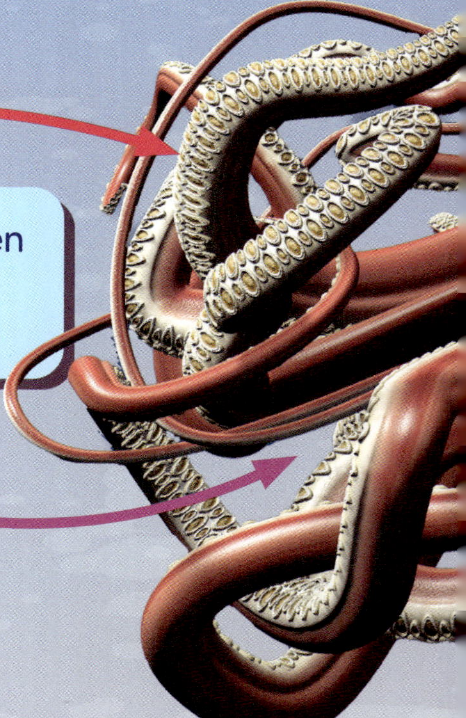

A parrot's beak

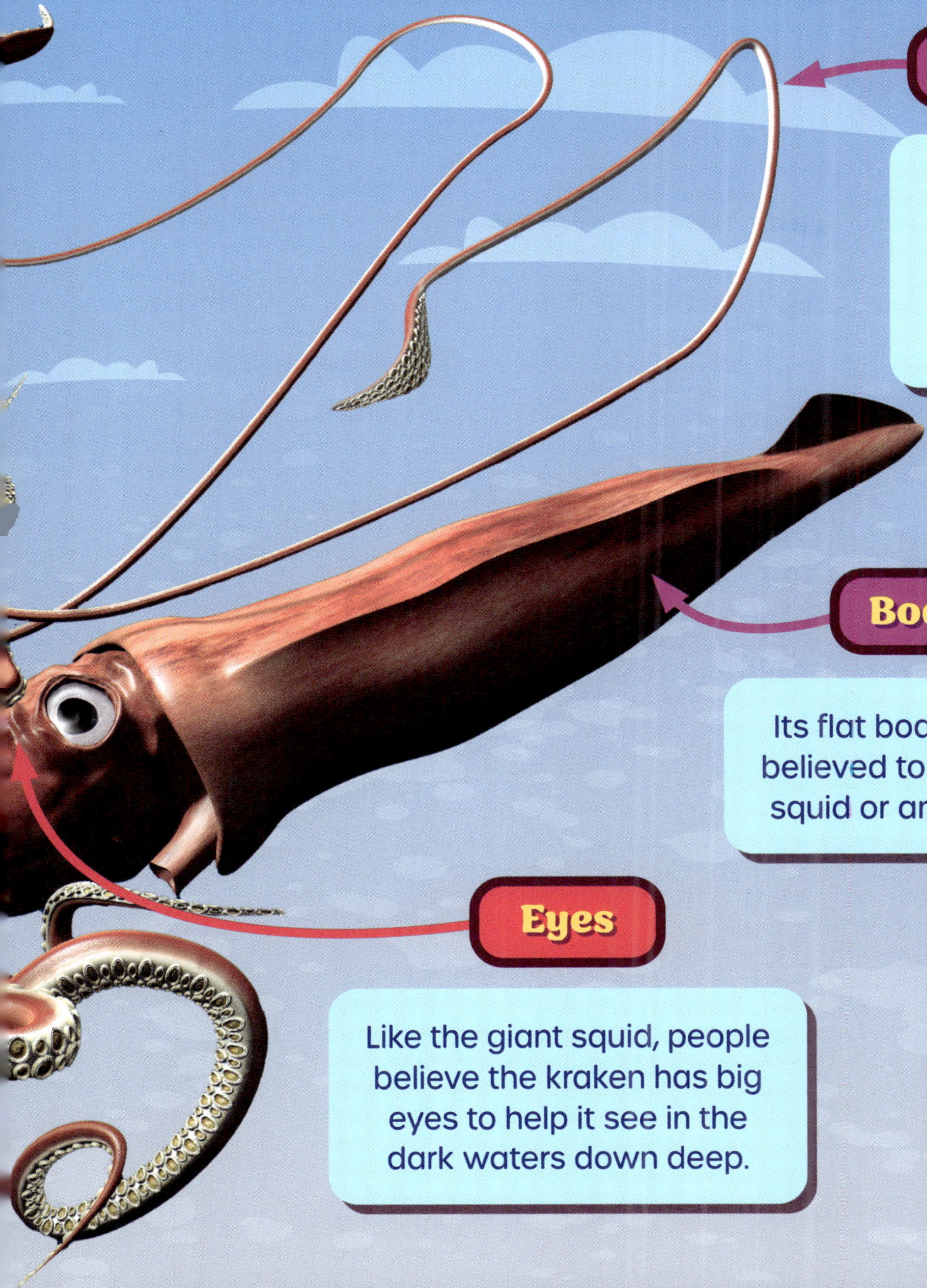

Tentacles

The kraken has two tentacles. These tentacles are longer than the arms.

Body

Its flat body is often believed to look like a squid or an octopus.

Eyes

Like the giant squid, people believe the kraken has big eyes to help it see in the dark waters down deep.

DEADLY ARMS

One of the most amazing things about the kraken is its powerful arms! Some say these limbs can be used to help the creature attack or build things.

Each arm has rows of strong suckers. These suckers can grab onto passing ships and drag them down into the deep sea.

In stories, the kraken builds its dens deep underwater. Octopuses make dens, too. Their dens are usually made of rocks. Could the kraken be **sinking** ships to use the **materials** on board for dens?

Dens are homes where animals rest, hide, or have young.

ONE OF A KIND

Apart from its deadly suckers, what else have we heard about this mythical creature? The kraken can make strong waves!

Most large ships can survive a whirlpool.

Some legends say the kraken can cause whirlpools. When diving into the ocean, this beast does not swim down calmly. It creates whirlpools powerful enough to pull ships under.

Some say the kraken is hundreds of years old. Maybe all the old stories are describing the same creature. Could the kraken be **immortal**?

THIS AND THAT

An orca

Legends say the kraken eats fish. Other sea creatures, such as orcas, also snack on fish.

In stories, the kraken is the size of an island. The largest known creature on Earth is the blue whale. Which one is bigger?

A blue whale

Most stories about the kraken come from sailors. What they say is hard to verify. That's because there are so many things out in the waters that have yet to be discovered. In fact, scientists have only explored five **percent** of the ocean.

About 71 percent of Earth's surface is covered by water.

SIGNS OF DANGER

When this powerful monster is nearby, stories say groups of fish start swimming away. Some fish may even jump out of the water in fear.

In legends, bubbling water is another sign that the kraken is close by. Maybe stormy weather and huge waves also start to appear. Could all these signs mean the kraken is coming?

Scientists have found more realistic explanations. Underwater **volcanoes** or other large sea creatures can cause bubbling water, too. Bad storms usually form from a mix of warm air and seawater.

WHERE THE KRAKEN LIVES

In many legends, the kraken lives in the waters near Norway and Iceland. But where exactly is it? Some say this sea beast must live in the deepest parts of the ocean there.

Does this mythical creature ever rise up to the surface? Stories say it comes only to feed or when the weather is warm.

The ocean is about 12,000 feet (3,600 m) deep.

MYTHICAL LOOK-ALIKES

There are other mythical creatures like the kraken. Let's take a look at a few.

A sea serpent

Sea serpents are described as huge snakes. Like the kraken, they are also said to cause trouble by sinking ships.

The Loch Ness monster is a mythical lake creature in Scotland. It is thought to have a long neck and two humps that come out of the water.

The Loch Ness monster

Scylla

Scylla (SIL-luh) is a sea monster from Greek **myths**. The creature has six monstrous heads and twelve tentacles. That's even more than the kraken!

REAL-LIFE KRAKEN?

Where do the stories of the kraken come from? Maybe from real animals. . . .

Oarfish

Oarfish are so long that people may have mistaken them for an arm or tentacle of the kraken. The longest oarfish ever recorded was 36 ft. (11 m) long.

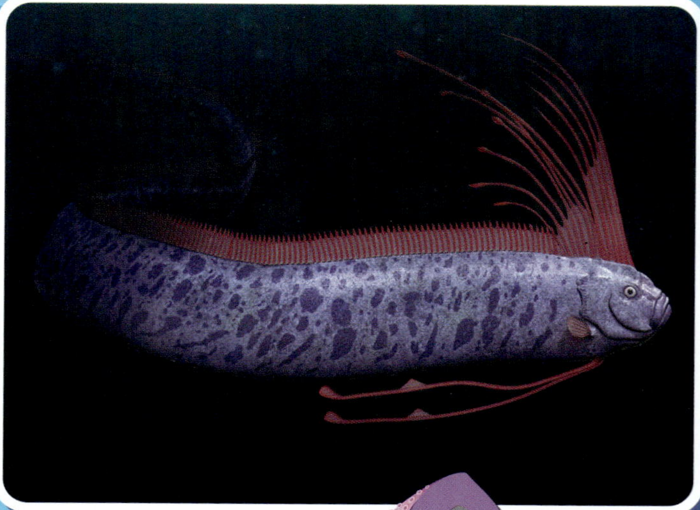

Giant Squid

Giant squids are often mistaken for the kraken. Like the kraken, giant squids do not often come to the surface. They can grow up to 43 ft. (13 m) long.

MYSTERIOUS MYTHICAL CREATURES

The kraken is a fun, mysterious creature. We can learn a lot from stories about this terrifying being.

If you can't get enough of the kraken, just read some books! There is so much to learn about this powerful, mythical creature.

Legends about the kraken go all the way back to 1180 CE.

GLOSSARY

immortal living or lasting forever

legends stories from the past that may have a mix of truth and made-up things

materials things that can be used to make something else

mythical based on stories or something made up in the imagination

myths stories that tell of strange or magical events and creatures

percent a part of a whole, expressed as a number out of 100

sinking moving downward toward the bottom of the ocean

volcanoes mountains that can send out rocks, ash, and lava in sudden explosions

INDEX